Shallow Thoughts

From An Empty Mind

A book of poems
Short stories
&
Narratives

By Chris Heigl

authorHOUSE®

AuthorHouse™
1663 Liberty Drive
Bloomington, IN 47403
www.authorhouse.com
Phone: 1-800-839-8640

Published by AuthorHouse 05/20/2016

ISBN: 978-1-4685-5107-5 (sc)
ISBN: 978-1-4685-5106-8 (hc)
ISBN: 978-1-4685-5105-1 (e)

Library of Congress Control Number: 2012902541

Print information available on the last page.

This book is printed on acid-free paper.

Shallow thoughts
From an empty mind.
I wade therein from time to time.
And though my thoughts are
really not that deep,
It's awfully hard to drownd in them
When thay only cover my feet.

Contents

Have You Seen This Woman Yet?

Have you seen this woman yet?
The one with style and grace,
Uniquely unavoidable, perfect in leather or lace.
Have you seen the way she moves?
She doesn't walk she stalks the room.
Severely in control, simply dangerous I'd say.
Have you met this woman yet?
She has a fragrance you won't forget,
And like a rose you'll stay to smell her sweet perfume.
Even when she's left the room.
If you meet this woman then, say hello for me,
But shield your heart or she'll steal it
away Just like she's done to me.

The First Time That I Saw You

The first time that I saw you,
I was filled with disbelief,
For I thought you were an angel,
As you glided down the street.
And I can't believe you did that to me.
And the first time that you ever said my name,
I was captured, held entranced,
And this is quite hard to explain,
But all I wanted was to hear you say
My name again.
And when you lay down by my side
I swear to God I thought I'd died,
And I knew then,
That I would never lie alone in bed again.
And when we pressed our lips in time,
I knew then that you'd be mine,
And we would be together for all eternity.
I still can't believe you did that to me.

Rat-A-Tat Tat

Rat-a-tat tat roars the concrete jack,
But still all I hear is you say,
"Darling, I think I'm in love with you",
And asking me if I feel the same way.
Oomff, POW, crack,
Goes the sledge hammers whack,
As I remember the words that I said.
"Sweetheart I know I'm in love with you,
From now till the day that I'm dead".
The dust how it flies,
How it clouds up the skies,
So I'm shocked when the dust settles down,
And I've found that I've carved
'I TRULY LOVE YOU'
On the ceiling the walls and the ground.

Sweetheart We Kiss

Sweetheart, we kiss,
We kiss and the world dissolves around me.
We hold each other tightly and nothing could tear us apart.
Our lives are intertwined and that keeps me from unraveling.
You are everything to me, my life, my love, my sweetheart.
Your touch, so gentle and soft you melt me.
Comforting, caring, caress.
Your beauty in my eyes is eternal,
If compared I would say you're the best.
Sweetheart we kiss.

Rose Petals

Rose petals envy your silky soft lips,
They taste just like wine,
Though far sweeter to kiss.
And all the worlds lilies
Would long for your skin,
Yet not one flower created
Could match your beauty within.

I Drink You Like Water

I drink you like water
Your sex is like rain
You drench my desires,
Like a flood fills the plain.
Your love is a well
That I drink from within,
My heart how it thirsts
For one sip of your skin.
Shower me with your passions,
Drowned me with your kiss,
Quench all of my desires
With a torrent of love
From your lips.

It's In Your Eyes

It's in your eyes,
The warmth of your touch,
The softness of your skin,
That makes me love you O' so much.
It's all the little things you say,
That make me think of you each day,
And all those special things you do,
That make me keep on loving you.
There was magic in the air
When you glanced in my direction
And all I did was stand and stare.
It seems my days are now complete
With you happily here in my life.
And I thought,
Wouldn't it be outstanding
If you wanted to be my wife?

The Cost of Loving You

What is the cost of loving you?
What is the price I should pay?
In order that I might stand next to you,
Hearing 'darling I love you' each day.
What do I owe you for having my child,
For creating a life in that way?
How much should I pay
For changing house into home,
And there in planning to stay?
The value of money is far less than your worth,
In fact it would take all the money on earth.
So in order to settle what I could never repay,
I've promised to love you
More and more every day.

So Quickly, So Suddenly

Is this the hand of God,
Are you my destiny,
Is this the way my life
Is really meant to be?
I am not blind
Though these things I cannot see.
Are you the one that heaven sent to me?
I was enslaved before you set my spirit free,
And this happened so very fast,
Almost naturally.
I am happier now than I ever thought I could be.
I really hope beyond all hope,
That you are my destiny.

This Woman

I've met this woman,
She's not a girl,
She's as different as gold is to a pearl.
She's not like anyone I've ever met before,
And now nothing seems to matter anymore.
I only want to feel her in my arms,
To feel her subtle charms,
And today there's only one thing I can say,
I hope to God that she never goes away.

Lust

Lust like one's own laughter
Is more human than divine.
It lasts but for a moment
Then quickly fades with time.
Love, true love is eternal
It can never be untied.
It has bound us all together
And will justify our lives.
Sometimes it is difficult to tell,
Which is lust and which is love,
But I've learned that if your patient,
God will guide you from above.
And if you're wise enough to wait,
On divine destiny,
I'll guarantee your happiness,
Throughout eternity.

Love, Lust And Passion

Don't confuse love, lust and passion.
Love is not lust, and lust should never
be confused with passion.
True love endures all tests of time.
True lust is the spark in one's heart
which lights the flame eternal.
True passion is the fuel on which our hearts will forever burn.
And love, true love is the vessel which
we keep forever deep inside,
Allowing us to live and have happiness
Together in both our lives.

Do not confuse love, lust and passion.
Lust is the spark that lights the flame,
Passion is the fuel that burns within,
And love is the vessel that holds the fire.

I Hold Your Hand

I hold your hand
And feel your soul is touching me,
Yes your soul touches me entirely.
In this I hope eternally.

We hug each other tightly
And I feel your spirit covers me,
Yes your spirit covers me entirely.
In this I hope eternally.

We kiss, and time just melts away.
You become a part of me,
I in you and you in me.
In this I hope eternally.

I hold your hand, your soul touches me.
We hug, your spirit covers me.
We kiss, you become a part of me.
In this I hope eternally.

I Didn't Ask

I didn't ask for you to save me.
I never wanted you to have my baby.
I didn't want you to save my life.
I never asked you to be my wife.
And if I did I'm sure you'd say I was crazy.
But even so I think you'd probably just say maybe.
I didn't ask, but I think you are the solution
Or at least some type of resolution,
To all of this confusion.

You

Your color, your texture, your taste.
The way your smile lights up your face.
Life is wonderful since the day that I met you.
And now everything is wonderful it's true.
Every little thing you do,
Is like magic in my eyes,
And all the simple things you say,
Always take me by surprise.
Things are so much better
Than they were just yesterday.
And I am truly grateful
I guess that's all I have to say.

I Know

I know exactly how you feel
Because my love for you is real.
And I'd love to hear you say
That you love me in the same way.
My life like yours had gone astray
And everything I had
Was lost or taken away.
But here you are today
And I would really like to say,
That I know exactly how you feel
Because my love for you is real.

With you I feel brand new.
The rain has stopped, my tears are gone
And the sun is shining brighter than it did just yesterday.
And there's one more thing I'd like to say,
I'm here to wipe your tears away.
Because my love for you is real,
And I know exactly how you feel.

A Woman's Body

A woman's body is made for a man.
From the time of his youth,
Lo from before he was born,
She has always been his woman.
He has always longed for her breast.
He has always longed for her form.
Her eyes, her lips, her hair,
Her erotic scent that fills the air.
When she is gone he feels nowhere.
But when she is there,
Therein he feels not a care.
And her lips, pressed against his skin,
There is healing powers yet within.
A simple touch, a simple kiss,
And yes this is all a man would miss,
As he dares to draw his last breath,
And think himself these things the best.

I Really Think I Understand

I really think I understand why a woman needs a man,
And a man does all he can to find a wife.
When God spit upon the ground then stirred the mud around,
And with his mighty breath he brought Adam to life.
Then with a rib from Adams side,
He formed a woman as Adams bride,
Named her Eve and Adam took her as his wife.
Ever since that faithful day, though
both of them had gone astray,
A man has longed for a woman to abide.
He feels complete with a woman by his side.

Baby You Drive Me Insane

Baby you drive me insane
With those sexy clothes you wear.
So beautiful blind men drop their canes
Turn around and stare.
And the way that you walk,
It makes the muted boys talk.
And the deaf listen in on every word that is said.
Your looks could wake the dead.
Baby you drive me insane.
You've affected my brain.
And there's nothing in this world
That I wouldn't do just to be with you.
And I know that the blind
and the deaf
and the mutes
and the dead
Would give anything right now,
If they could be with you too.

Chapter 2

Love Lost

Every Day I Lay My Heart Down

Every day I lay my heart down at your feet,
Because you're lovely kind and sweet,
And every day you gently move it to the side and walk on by,
Still every day I try.
Every day I try to show you how I feel,
Because my love for you is real,
And every day you kindly smile and walk on by,
Still every day I try.
So every day when you see me do the same as yesterday,
Know that I'll keep trying,
Because I love you every day,
And tomorrow I will love you even more than yesterday.

How Can I Abandon True Love?

How can I abandon true love?
Relinquishing my passions,
Surrendering my dreams,
Abolishing God's blessings,
And all that they would bring.
How could I be absolved of all these things?
How could I turn my face from loving you?
For as God so loved the world,
Though each one of us is yet untrue.
How could I abandon true love,
And turn my face from you?
No I choose to forgive all of your sins.
I absolve you of your transgressions
And all you've ever been.
For the sake of love I choose to vindicate,
As the admission of love is at stake.
And nothing but love is valued as great.
Truly how could I stop loving you?

A Diamond Is Of No Value

A diamond is of no value.
It cannot shine on its own.
It cannot grow to feed the poor,
nor shelter or keep them warm.
It's naturally misshapen
And must be ground to form.
It seems its only propose
Is to ultimately be worn.
My love is like a diamond,
I'd hoped you'd cherish it.
I offered it for you to wear,
And hoped that it would fit.
But you took my love for granted,
And then you gave it back,
Saying "This is just a big clear rock,
Now where's the value in that?"

It's Not The Way She Looks

It's not the way she looks,
Though the way she looks
Is way beyond compare.
It's the way she looks at you,
And the way she looks at you
Is rather like a stare.
I wonder what she's thinking,
Because what she's really thinking
Is something way out there.
I want to know what she knows.
Because I know that she knows
What I know and she really doesn't care.
I like to go over there because when I do,
I'm over hear and she's over there,
And she looks at me with that stare
That say's "I really don't care."

A Bird Is To A Cat

It's like a bird is to a cat,
A spider and a fly,
I have fallen for your trap,
Entangled prey am I.
For you to do with as you will,
A petty toy am I.
Something more to be amused,
To let survive or die.
You delight in my reactions,
And how powerful are you.
And how pitiful am I,
To let you tell me what to do.
You are like an addiction,
To me you are a need,
You are the only substance,
That my mind and body feed.
And just like an addiction,
You're in my garden like a weed.

I Wonder What You're Thinking

I wonder what you're thinking,
When you look in to my eyes?
If what was true came shining through,
We both would be surprised.
I wonder what you're thinking?
I'd really like to know.
Because whatever you are thinking,
Never seems to show.
Are you happy?
Are you sad?
Are you lonely?
Are you mad?
Why is it that you never ever smile?
Understanding what's in your head
Is going to take a while.

Something That Stands Between Us

I love you,
Yet there's something that stands between us,
Like I'm on the planet Mars,
And you're on the planet Venus.
Sometimes I feel that you're a million miles away.
We are as far apart as night time is to Day.
I love you,
But there's something not copasetic,
And I am sure that we'll regret it.
Though I really wish this wasn't true,
There is nothing this world could do,
To make me stay with you.
I love you.
And though are hearts are far away,
And our minds and souls have gone astray,
We're still a million miles away.
And that's how it's going to stay,
I guess we're better off that way.

You Prick, You Dick

You Prick, you Dick,
You low life piece of Shit.
I've no idea what you're thinking,
But what I do know makes me sick.
Everything about you,
Every single thing you do,
Shows me that you're total scum,
And everyone knows it's true.
You're the lowest form of life on earth,
They should have put you back at birth.
You're the reason that I own a gun.
Normally I'd shoot you just for fun.
Just one bullet in the head,
Your mom would thank me when you're dead.
Your slimier than spit,
You low life piece of shit.

Liar, Liar Pants On Fire

Liar, liar, pants on fire.
Every single thing you said,
And all those things you used to do,
Not one single thing about you,
Was even close to true.
I don't even think you even know yourself.
You never move from here to there,
Without some sort of stealth.
What were you before,
Before you turned into a lying whore?
Were you ever someone beautiful?
Because you're not that any more.
Liar, liar, pants on fire.
You're really just a slut.
And you will always be that way,
Always, no matter what.

You Lied

You said that you loved me.
You lied.
You said that you'd never hurt me,
But then you made me cry.
You said that your love would never stray,
But then one day you went away.
You said that you loved me.
You lied.
You said you'd always be with me,
And we'd be together eternally.
But now that you've gone,
I know I was wrong.
You said that you loved me,
You lied.

I'm Tired

I'm tired of being in places that I know you'll never be.
I'm tired of writing poems that I know you'll never see.
I'm tired of never knowing what I'm not supposed to do.
I'm tired so very tired of being alone and without you.
Often people wonder why I'm crying all the time,
It's because I think I love you and I'm not sure if you're mine.
You said you loved me truly, and in this I have no fear,
But if you love me truly,
Why then aren't you here?

The stars in the sky

I would like to give you the stars in the sky
But I can't even give you the moon up above.
I would like to be the gleam in your eye
But I can't even touch the tip of your love.
It's utterly amazing how deeply I care for you
And more utterly amazing is there's nothing I can do.

In The Garden

I walked within the garden,
And each flower is beautiful it's true.
But none of these lovely flowers
Are half as beautiful as you.
Their colors are painted brightly
And nothing looks out of place,
But their colors pale when they are compared
To the beauty of your face.
I love to be in the garden
With all the beauty that I see,
But I'd love it even more
If you were standing here with me.

You Violated My Dreams

You violated my dreams.
I think you know what I mean.
The minute you got inside my brain,
All you did was drive me insane.
It's not the words you choose,
It's the tone of voice you used.
It's not the look in your eyes,
It's the fact that you lied.
And the minute you got inside my head,
I swear to God I wish I was dead.
And now there is nothing that I can do,
Because I'm still in love with you.

Smoldering Embers

Smoldering embers gave birth to a fire
Whom when joined with the wind grew even higher,
And they danced O' Lord how they danced.
The wind loved the flame he surrounded her so,
She relied on his presence and more brightly did glow.
And they danced O' Lord how they danced.
The warmth of the flame and her beautiful glow
Was now tied to the wind no matter which way he'd blow.
And they danced O' Lord how they danced.
But the fire is fickle and so is the breeze,
For as quickly as it started it then died with such ease.
But they danced O' Lord how they danced.

I Think Your Lips Are Made Of Wine

I think your lips are made of wine.
You intoxicate me with every kiss.
And now that you have gone away,
Your kiss is what I miss.
O to feel your lips upon my face,
The warmest I'll ever know.
How could I have been so stupid to have ever let you go?
They say kisses are sweeter than honey,
But your kisses my dear are like wine.
And each day that I think of your kisses,
They seem sweeter all the time.

Like A Chinese Box

That woman was just like a Chinese box.
I spent years trying to get in.
And when I finally solved the puzzle,
I found that there was nothing inside at all.
I expected more because
Tthe outside was so beautifully carved.
With all that decorated wood
Painted with such bright colors.
It was so wonderfully complex.
I really thought there would be
Something on the inside,
But no. Nothing...
Just emptiness.

Your Beauty Blinded Me

Your beauty blinded me to the dreadful reality
Of the truth I simply could not see.
Our love was really never meant to be.
Others saw it plain as day, but not me.
Well, really, what can I say?
I guess my life just goes that way.

They say all broken hearts will mend with time.
And So I will always consider you
A close personal friend of mine.
Let me then bid you a fond adieu,
And hope someday to meet you
Somewhere around the bend.
In the end, Good will to you I'll send.
Adieu, adieu, goodbye my friend.

Chapter 3

Broken Hearted

My Heart

My heart has been utterly broken.
It's shattered beyond all repair.
And I can see clearly inside of it,
And I see that there's nothing in there.
No wonder I have no emotions.
No love nor sorrow, just despair.
No pleasure nor purpose nor ecstasy,
Quite simply there's nothing in there.
My heart my heart, my poor broken heart,
Without it I live quite in vain.
And without the passion that once there did lie,
I feel living my life is in vain.

The Love Of My Life

The love of my life is like a rose.
Her beauty is perfection,
Her fragrance fills the air,
To have her there then next to me,
I've therein not a care.
But, to possess her, no, to take her,
And then to make her mine.
To hold her beauty tightly,
Though seemingly divine.
Would cause such pain and suffering
That I'm obliged to warn,
That blood will flow
Least from your heart,
Let run by all her thorn.

I Don't Understand

I don't understand how you can love someone
With all your heart and soul.
How is it possible to feel so much for someone else?
So much that you can't even see the other person.
You can't see what they are doing.
You can't hear what they are saying.
You can't fathom how evil they are.
And you're so in love that it doesn't even matter.
I don't understand it at all.
And when it's over,
I don't understand why there has to be so much pain.
You begin to see how they deceived you.
You begin to learn about all the lies.
You fathom how evil they are.
And it still hurts.
I don't understand.

Never Fall in Love

I will never fall in love again.
It's not because love is a sin,
It's the pain that it causes,
It's the hurt deep within.
I do not care what others say,
I will never fall in love again.
Not tomorrow, not next year,
And certainly not today.

I Wish

I wish I had a gun.
Then I could erase the awful truth from my mind,
And go back to believing every word that you said.
Why aren't you laying here next to me?
Why aren't you here in my bed?
Why have you left me in missery?
"Im leaving" is all that you said.
Ouch, my heart.
Ouch, my mind.
Ouch my soul is dead.

Is Anybody Really Happy

Is anyone really happy?
Does anyone really care?
Is anything that important?
Is anything ever fair?
All my life I've suffered,
Nothing here is for free,
There's nothing left to live for,
But pain and misery.
Is anyone really happy?
Does anyone give a damn?
Is anything worth the price we pay?
Is anything according to plan?
All My life is full of strife,
Nothing goes my way,
There's nothing here worth having,
There's nothing left to say.

Reality Is Misery

When the sun rises and I open my eyes,
Reality is misery.
I remember those days, it makes me cry.
Misery, my misery.
I cannot change, I'm too weak to try.
Misery, poor misery.
You see me smile, but it's all a lie.
Misery, can't you see?
My heart is in pain, I want to die.
Misery, set me free.
And If I jump, I'm sure I'll fly.
Say goodbye to misery.

When Something's Broken

When something is broken,
It usually takes a long time to put it back together.
Sometimes, it cannot be repaired at all.
Other times it is fixable,
But will be missing a few pieces.
Often, it won't work properly,
And the damage it's suffered will show.
Most of the time when something is broken,
It will never be the same again.
So take care not to break the things around you.
Try not to damage those things that
you find precious and dear.
And most of all protect your heart,
For it breaks the easiest I fear.

The Emptiness Inside

I can feel the emptiness inside,
Now that you have left me all alone.
There is no need for you to run and hide,
No pressing questions to abide.
No need for you to lie.
All that love and adoration
Can now be put aside.

As I stand here by myself,
Knowing you will not arrive,
And all those plans for happiness,
Have gone and passed me by.
My heart pumps pain and longing,
And I suffer without you.
Now that you have gone away,
Being alone is all I do.

Try and Console

Do not try to console me,
Or stand here by my side.
The pain will not abide itself,
I live but want to die.

They say it's better without you,
And though I know it's true,
I still feel pain and loneliness,
Now that I am without you.

I'm sorry dear, I want you here.
It's lonely without you.

I Hate Your Guts

I hate your guts you piece of shit!
You're so damn mean you make me sick.
I cannot stand to see you in the light of day.
You're so damn ugly even spiders run away.
I'd really like it if you got hit by ten Mac trucks.
But I still love you, and boy that really sucks.

The Sorcery

The sorcery of a woman
Will turn proud kings to fools.

She will make an honest man lie
And the handsome man feel buffooned.

The sorcery of a woman
Will turn the upstanding to shame.

She will make a smart man ignorant
And the wild man then restrained.

The sorcery of these women,
With their sultry voice and sensual ways,

Are devised for men to become ensnared,
And then ultimately enslaved.

Death

Death,
Do not hide your face from me,
Come take away my misery.
For to die would be less painful,
Than living could ever be.
Oh to die and then to lay at rest,
To end this suffering.
For the pain of my heart is far greater,
Then dying could ever be.
But, 'how to die?' I ask myself,
And escape this misery.
How to lay myself at rest,
Lo death come near to me.

A Leaky Boat

My life is like a leaky boat,
Tossed upon the sea.
All my friends and family,
Have long abandoned me.
I've thought of putting into port,
And seeking some repair,
But this leaky boat is floundering,
And seems to go nowhere.
I need someone to stay with me,
Who can endure all of this wrath.
Someone who sees a leaky boat,
And wants to take a bath.

Chasing Happiness

I feel as though I'm chasing Happiness around the Tree of Life.
I wonder if I stop if Happiness will run into me?

Chapter 4

Addiction

My Own Addiction

I am my own addiction,
I have enslaved myself.
I choose to ingest poisons that would liquidate my health.

And though no chains are visible,
Nor bars do surround me.
I am in fact a prisoner and my mind won't set me free.

I've asked for some reprisals,
Or at least a small reprieve,
But this drug won't hear the pardon
so my mind won't let me be.

It's easier to stay enslaved,
And endure this misery,
Than to quit this drug and admit that's it and end this tragedy.

Your Sorrow

Your sorrow has obscured the light
that glows within your heart.
It casts a pitch black shadow, making all your life seems dark.
And so you've learned to live your life
that's filled with such disdain,
That you choose to ingest drugs and
booze to ease all of the pain.

And though you think these things you do
Will somehow help you through,
Someone should let you know right now,
These things are killing you.

So if you'd like a little help,
Too somehow see you through,
Just think of these three little words,
Remember "I love you".

Because Of An Addiction.

I run to those things I do not love,
I run away from those that love me most.
All because of an addiction.

I'm in love with what is not real,
And what gives me the most love I can barely feel.
All because of an addiction.

I've disappointed everyone including me,
And who it is that I've become, I simply cannot see.
All because of an addiction.

Life has granted me an abundance of freedom,
But I've chosen bonds of misery.
All because of an addiction.

Will I always be this way?
From where I'm at today I truly can not say.
All because of an addiction.

The Addictions Of My Flesh

The addictions of my flesh
Lacerate my brain.
My life is uncontrollable
I am somewhat insane.
The weakness of my will
And the poisons I digest,
Liquidate my body
And bring on an early death.

My Addictions

Oppression lives within my addictions,
It drains me of all my convictions.
I drown within my past, my sins.
Why should I run a race I cannot win?

I am the conductor of my life.
I am the orchestrator of my strife.
And though living, I long to feel.
My heart is damaged and will not heal.

Oh I speak the truth that my happiness is vanquished,
That spark of life has languished.
I feel that the soft light of life has left me,
And even so, nothing I do is heavenly or worthy of eternity.

Truly my oppression lives within my addictions,
It drains me of all my convictions.
I drown within my past, my sins.
Why should I run a race I cannot win?

The Errors

The errors of my life,
The mistakes and oversights,
The misappropriations of my deeds,
And through it all from rise to fall
It's me I have deceived.

So here I sit and wonder,
I count my blunders and I grieve.
I ponder then unto myself
What will become of me.

How will others view my life
When I am history?
Is this the life that God had planned
When he created me?
Or have I tarnished what was right
And brought on this tragedy?

Takers and Givers

The takers and the givers,
The winners and the thieves,
The lovers and the haters,
The joyful and bereaved.
The saviors and betrayers,
The powerless and the strong,
The sinners and the righteous,
The one who's right,
And the one who's wrong.

And I'm there in the middle,
Not on the left nor right,
Not giving up entirely,
Nor do I wish to fight.
I'm solidly in-between it all,
One foot on either side,
Trying my best to stay at bay,
And enjoying what's left of my high.

A Monkey On Your Back

Sin is not a monkey on your back,
It's more like maggots in your underwear.
A monkey lives in the open,
Can be trained and lives as a pet.
A maggot hides itself,
Eats away the flesh and causes decay.
A monkey is cute and furry.
A maggot is entirely repulsive.
A monkey can reproduce,
Belongs to a family and can nurture.
Maggots are the result of
Equally repulsive creatures
Which in themselves cause disease and decay.
They exist only to be devoured,
Cleverly ensnared as food
For other more notable creatures.
The funny thing is people know
That they have maggots in their pants
And they choose to live with it.
They seek out other people
Who also have maggots in their pants to hang out with.

Let me tell you, sin is not a monkey on your back,
It's a handful of maggots in your underwear.

In The Land Of Harm

In the land of harm,
Those with small minds and short tempers
Stand on the heads of the weak and the weary,
So that they may arise
And look down on those beneath them.

Don't Look At Me

Don't look at me I can't be seen, I'm hiding in the sky.
Don't bring me down, not on the ground, it all can't be a lie.
This shiny space won't leave a trace
of what you've been or seen.
Its common rule to stay awake, for if not it's a dream.

Life of Strife

Life, Life so full of strife,
And there go I,
Like a blind man,
Leaving a burning building.

Such A Waste To Me

Everything seems such a waste to me, The forest and
jungles and things in the sea, It's like chasing your shadow
up under a tree, And it all seems a waste to me.
Life breeds in abundance but why? The plants and
the trees grow old and then die, Animals breed then
are eaten alive, It all seems a waste to me.
I live by myself over here, While billions of others
survive over there, And when it's all over we really
don't care, And it all seems a waste to me.
We all strive for a life filled with pleasure, While each
one of us causes such pain. It's never made much of a
difference, And in fact it all feels quite the same.
So what if I share and you won't? So what if you care
and I don't. To me life seems such a waste, The only real
meaning is to take up space. It all seems a waste to me.

Distraction

The TV distracts me.
The radio distracts me.
You tend to distract me.
Distractions to distract us.
Isn't there something we could do?
Something not as hard?
Distractions causing fatalities.
Something more relaxing?
Distractions causing deaths.
Something where I can sit down.
Distractions killing time.
Maybe you'd like to join me?
Distractions cost billions,
It only lasts a couple hours.
Distractions to distract us.
Everything we do is a distraction.
But distract us from doing what?

When I Was Young

Back when I was young,
Everything was so fun,
And the future was going to be so bright,
They told me everything was going to be all right.
But then I grew old and I just seemed to lose my hold,
And all these things that I was never told,
Just seemed to be happening to me.
All the pain and suffering
And the tears that this life brings,
All the broken hearts and shattered dreams.
Life is never what it seems.
When I was young they lied.
I guess they lied so I would try
To make it through this life filled with pain.
For the truth be known, the future shown,
We all will suffer the same,
And we only have ourselves to blame.

Girl In a Beat Up World

She was a beat up girl in a beat up world,
Her mother made love at the wrong time, in the wrong place,
To the wrong man, and nine months later she was born.
Her daddy left when she was only two.
Her mommy will remarry very soon.
Because she didn't know what else to do.
Her new daddy loved her very, very much.
He made love to her anytime he could get away with it.
Her mother had changed her cigarette brands three times,
But pretty much stayed with gin throughout the rest of her life.
Remarkably, invisibly, the girl grew up and finished school.
She got a job and went to work each day.
It really doesn't matter how this story ends.
Nobody knows, nobody cares,
It won't matter to anybody but her.

Sorcery

Sorcery
Like drugs
Has had an effect on me.
I've lost control of who I was
And what I used to be.

I do not look at all the same,
I act so differently.
I once was strong but now I'm week.
Once in control now shy and meek.

That thing that once was so important to me,
Has now become a distant memory.

Those people that I used to long to see before,
I think it's safe to say that they won't see me anymore.

And that lovely one and only until the day I die,
Doesn't want me anymore and it's all because of my lie.

Sorcery
Like drugs,
Like falling in love with a whore.
All of these things hold dangers for me
That I've never known before.

Stop Digging.

You reach the bottom when you stop digging.
The deeper the hole you've dug,
The harder it is to climb out of.

Sometimes you've gotten so far down,
That there is simply no way out.
You can either sit there and do nothing,
Or you can start digging again.
Hoping someday to reach the end
Or the bottom or the other side.

The trick in life is to stop digging,
Before you've gotten in too deep,
In above your head,
Beyond your ability to escape
From the hole you've dug.

Angry

Angry
Neurotic
Psychotic
In pain

Homicidal
Suicidal
Genocide
Untamed

Addicted
Vindictive
Convicted
Inflamed

Certifiable
Undeniable
Indescribable
Insane

And so goes this letter from me to a friend,
We wish you a Merry Christmas
And hope for the end.

Chapter 5

Recovery

That's It I Quit

That's it, I quit,
I cannot handle it.
I've reached the end of this rope so long ago,
My hands are tired and my arms are weak
And I really must let go.

And as I've set my mind and body free,
I'm quite surprised to find,
What's happening to me?
For instead of falling down,
And plunging to the ground,
I find I'm actually rising,
As my life has turned around.

I thought if I'd let go I'd surely die,
But the moment that I freed myself,
That's when I learned I could fly.
Let's hope you understand what I've said is true,
So you'll let go and free yourself,
From the rope you hang onto.

Bridges

I've burned a lot of bridges,
Some thick some long some wide,
And rebuilding a lot of these bridges,
Seems to take so very much time.
The most difficult thing about rebuilding a bridge,
That is to say the hardest part,
Is not in the shape or the length to the width,
It's gathering enough courage to start.

I Am Also A Spirit

I am also a spirit dwelling here in flesh and bone,
And in this lust filled animal my spirit makes its home.
This animal, of which I am, the one that others call a man,
Seeks nothing but to satisfy itself.
And so I find it spends it's time destroying its own health.
And otherwise it's occupied accumulating wealth.
But my spirit sits there quietly observing everything.
It is silent and it's peaceful and it rarely intervenes.
Sometimes when the day is done,
When my body's tired and had its fun.
My spirit makes its way inside my head saying,
"Keep this up and you will soon be dead".
It seems to me that's all my spirits ever really said.

Black wax

So I asked my lord,
How can I remove this black waxy sin that covers my hands?
Already so thick that it binds my fingers together,
Preventing me from feeling anything at all.
I tried washing it on Sundays but it was to no avail.
I tried melting it with fire but it only ran down upon my arms.
I tried rubbing it away, but it only spread.
I tried ignoring it however others noticed it for me.
I tried everything it seems but nothing would set me free.
So I asked my lord the way to remove
this sin from off my skin.
He said he'd told me how before but I did not listen to him.
I said I hadn't asked before, he said that others like you did.
I said, had the others found the cure?
He said, Most ran away and hid.
I asked, where are the others now?
He said, they all are dead.
Is there none left living?
"No" is all he said.
This cure I'm sure is costly.
He said he'd paid the price.

He said he'd suffered at Calvary and that he gave his life.
For me he gave his life away so I could live again.
And live on throughout eternity,
A life that's without sin.
I said, I believe what you said is true,
But what would you have me to do?
He said, Go tell the others,
And when they'd ask, he'd clean them too.

We grow

If we care for ourselves we will grow,
And the blossoms and fruit we produce,
Will more than plainly show.
If we dwell within the darkness
And not out in the light,
Then the blossoms and the fruits
Will probably not look right.
If we constantly tend to our
Most basic needs, then the blossoms
And fruits we produce will cast seeds.
It's right that all life is designed this way,
So the fruitful grow and the others decay.
It's a simple truth and is so plain to see,
The plants and the trees are just like you and me.

Change

I've changed,
Thank God I've changed,
Everything about me
I've completely rearranged.

All the things I used to do,
I've done them all before,
And now I swear to God
I just don't want that any more.

So now that it's true,
Let's hope you too,
Don't want that any more.
Let's say we've changed.

Let's both say it,
"I've changed"

Godly men

Lord help us in our covenant
To live as Godly men.
To keep us and protect us
And deliver us from sin.
Each one of us is human,
Which causes us to stray.
Lord guide us and protect us,
That we may find our way.
Without our lord and savior,
Our hearts were full of strife.
But since you came
And died for me,
I have eternal life.
Lord help us and protect us.
Please change us from within.
Help us all to find our way,
And to live as Godly men.

Every Single Step

Every single step I take
On the path in front of me,
Is further from who I once was
Yet closer to whom I'll be.
Although my change is visible
It's not for all to see,
For changing all I ever was
Starts first inside of me.
So if you try to recognize
The person I've become,
Try looking deep inside of me
And know I've just begun.

I Closed My Eyes And Wandered

I closed my eyes and wandered.
I wandered aimlessly.
My view was skewed with drugs and booze,
So in fact I could not see.
I wandered past my lovers,
Past my friends and family.
I could not find my own way back,
So I wandered aimlessly.

I did not know where I would go,
Where I'd been nor who I'd see.
I did not know who I'd become,
Or what would become of me.

But today I stopped and looked around,
I saw my footprints on the ground,
And I could see the path I'd taken.
Tinny little circles that went
Around,
and Around and Around.

Dewdrop

As night time yields unto the day,
A dewdrop forms then slips away,
And adds itself unto this thing called life.

Just as life renews itself again,
With every dew drops flight.
I'm reminded we can start anew,
And therein do what is right.

A new day dawns,
A dew drop falls,
And in the mornings light,
My life can thus begin again,
And everything is right.

Tiniest Bubble

From the deepest darkest waters,
Even the tiniest bubble shall rise.
This analogy, though not plain to see,
Reminds me of years gone by.
Our lives are out of our control,
But if we choose to do what's right,
We're destined to rise above it all,
And arrive into the light.

Your Cup

Is it half full or half empty?
Do you know which is true from within?
Is the contents contained soon to dissipate,
Or about to flow over the rim?
Are you patiently waiting for good times ahead?
Or dreading the days in your path till you're dead?
Do you know which is true at this half-way mark?
Is your life soon complete,
Or is this just the start?

Here Within

Here within myself,
I find the answers to every question that I have yet to ask.

Deep inside myself,
I can see past all the lies,
Through all the layers of my intricate disguise.

Looking deep inside myself,
I come to realize,
That the answer to every question to every mystery on earth,
Is buried deep inside myself,
It's been this way from birth.

Here inside myself,
I find everything I need to understand just who I am,
And who I'm really supposed to be.

Chapter 6

Children

I Remember Before

I remember before I was lost,
But now I am here my dear.
I am here in the night
When you wake from a fright,
My shoulder is here for your head.
My gentlest kisses are here for your cheek,
As I gently place you back in bed.
I am here to dry off your wet body,
As you're finally done with your bath.
I am patiently here smiling back at you,
As you constantly giggle and laugh.
I am here to bandage your scrapes and your scuffs
Whenever you have fallen down.
I am here to tell you I love you,
Whenever your knee hits the ground.
I am here to tell you I love you,
or give you a great big kiss,
I am here whenever you're lonely,
I am here and will never be missed.
I truly remember being lost before,
But, I am not lost any more.
I am right here, where I'm supposed to be,
And right here, I will always be.

A Deep Breath

Take a deep breath and count to ten,
That is the first rule of discipline.
Although you are angry, try not to shout,
Remember its boundaries you're talking about.
Don't raise your hand, never hit pinch or shove,
Keep in your mind, it's all about love.
Focus your words, direct what you say,
Your children will likely treat others that way.
When your children are grown having kids of their own,
You'll be glad that they've learned to show love in their home.

What Are You Doing Son?

What are you doing son?
Just building rocket ships for fun.
Do you think you might need some tape or glue?
Nope, this nail right here should do.
What's that small hole for, above the fin?
That's where me and my sister get in.
When do you two plan on flying away?
After my lunch and naptime I'd say.
How long do you both plan on being gone?
Just to the moon and back, not very long.
I believe you, my son, for when I was yet five,
I remember quite clearly, that I knew how to fly.

My Christmas Tree

My Christmas Tree never looked this tall,
The colors were never that bright.
The lights that I've used year after year,
Never seemed to sparkle at night.
But now that my children are here,
This Christmas is dripping with cheer.
The presents and stockings all light up their eyes,
Everything's new and such a surprise.
And those time honored lyrics,
To those old Christmas songs,
I find myself smiling and singing along.
I used to be sad on this holiday season,
But now I am glad being sad has no reason.
Now that my children are here,
This Christmas is dripping with cheer.

Liar

I've turned into a liar. I lie every day.
I lie and say, "Yes," when my son asks,
"Do you know what I say?"
"Do you remember (blah, blah, blah and so on)"
And, of course I say, "Yes" and keep driving along.
It's not that I'm deaf or am tuning him out,
I just can't understand what he's talking about.
So, every day, I will listen, and every day, I will try,
Because soon, he'll be older, then I won't have to lie.

Bold Two Year Old

I've never met a woman quite as bold,
As my darling little two year old.
She defies the laws of gravity,
As easily as she does me.
She'll scale the highest high chair,
As fast as a squirrel climbs a tree.
Her crib playpen and car seat,
Are escaped quite easily,
And regardless of their invention,
Her goal is to be set free.
A magician would be in envy,
And Houdini put to shame,
For the strongest ribbon,
and tightest bows,
Are cast off like locks and chains.
It's hard to be frustrated,
By all her wily deeds,
For even though she's only two,
She's so much smarter than me.

My Son

Within seconds, my son, who is so very young,
Can find one ton of trouble where before there was none.
That brown paper bag that I've brought from the store,
Now contains broken glass where there was none before.
And that small cardboard box that arrived in the mail,
Either contains his sister or has learned how to wail.
This mischievous demon that's so small and weak,
Will soon turn into an angel when he's then fast asleep.
So I'm done with his feeding and bathing and bed,
I'll try yet to slumber, for tomorrow I dread.

From Your Father

You got it from your father,
It was all he had to give,
So it's yours to use and cherish,
For as long as you may live.
If you lose the watch he gave you,
It can always be replaced,
But a black mark on your name,
Can never be erased.
It was clean the day you took it,
And a worthy name to bear,
When he got it from his father,
There was no dishonor there.
So make sure you guard it wisely,
After all is said and done,
You'll be glad the name is spotless,
When you give it to your son.

Sleepy Head

Good morning sleepy head,
Time to get out of bed.
Now, be a good princess,
Let's get dressed and get fed.
Let me change your wet diapers,
Powder and wipe,
Let me pin back your hair,
What bow would you like?
Is this the right color?
Is that the right shade?
Please try to hold still,
Please do not run away.
I'm tying my best to meet every need,
But try as I might all you do is flee.
Do you want to be naked for the rest of the day?
Then please come back here and do what I say.
Being a father means all work and no play,
Fulfilling your needs day after day.
I have no idea why God made us this way,
It's fun, that's for sure,
Now, let's have a nice day.

My Children Today

What have I learned from my children today?
Well they both seem much older than they were yesterday.
My three year old speaks quite a lot, as it seems,
While I hear every word, I'm not sure what he means.
And my cute little girl, who is one and a half,
Follows me everywhere, even into the bath.
I guess what I've learned, what I'm trying to say,
Is to cherish tomorrow, it won't be like today.
We all seem much older than we were yesterday.

A Tree

What's that? It's a tree.
What's that? It's a tree.
What's that? It's another tree son.
As I smile and try to remember,
When I thought having children was fun.
What's that? It's a tree.
What's that? It's a tree.
What's that? It's a tree.
Now stop bothering me!
What's that? It's a tree.
What's that? It's a tree.
What's that? It's another tree son.
And that's when I'm shocked
As I look down the road,
Oh, my God, there are hundreds of them!

Boundaries

What's in your mouth?
What's in your hand?
Why don't you put that away?
Don't do that, you'll break your neck!
Please, just do what I say.
Boundaries don't come naturally
To children under three.
My job is to keep them from hurting themselves,
In the meantime, it's killing me.

I Wear A Smile

I wear a smile a lot more than before,
My children have attached it in place.
Before I had worn my smile upside down,
But now it's upright on my face.
It is there first thing in the morning,
As my daughter shouts," DADDY!" at me.
I smile and change her wet diapers,
As she happily smiles back at me.
I smile as my son says he's superman,
Then jumps up and goes tearing around.
I smile and thank God for my children,
Who turned that old frown upside down.

Noodles And Such

You know, feeding my children noodles and such,
Reminds me of life, so very much.
Each meal that I made would seem a success,
Yet, when it was over, I found it a mess.
So, try as I might, to keep my kids clean,
It was just a disaster, if you know what I mean.
Like life, eating noodles is so very much fun.
So enjoy it, get messy, like when you were young.

Rollie Polies

Rollie Polies, Dandelions and bubbles in the air,
All these things I look right through,
But my children stop and stare.
Rain drops cause bewilderment
To a two year old.
To me, it seems so bothersome.
I guess I'm just too old.
Is that a bus?
Is that a truck?
"Daddy, is that a train?"
My three year old just has to know,
But, to me, they're all the same.
I seldom stop to ponder,
Or to let my mind wander.
I just don't seem to have a child's brain.
I guess you'd say I'm all grown up.
Now, isn't that a shame?

Chapter 7

God

You've Done It Again

You've done it again,
Laid waste to an innocent man.
You're concert of accusations,
Have gone exactly as you've planned.
Beat him, make him suffer,
Tear the beard from off his face.
Mock him, try and shock him,
That will put him in his place.
For blasphemy and heresy,
The man deserves to die.
Take him up to Calvary,
Choose him to Crucify.
And as he hung upon the cross,
Thorns upon his head,
Day turned to night,
The sky went dark,
The son of God was dead.
You've done it again,
Laid waste to an innocent man.

We Exist

Did we exist before we existed?
Were we something more before?
Did we live before we breathed?
And is there something more in store?
On and on goes the debate,
To exist without an existence
In another time and space.
To live before life,
to see without eyes.
Maybe up in the clouds,
Way up high in the sky.
I don't think we'll ever know,
Which way we're soon to go.
Is it up or down?
Left or right?
Is it eternal darkness?
Or everlasting light?
Did we exist before we existed?
And do we exist after this life?

Strength Today

Lord Give me strength today.
Please keep me safe and help me find my way.
Guide my steps so I won't stray,
Protect me each and every day.
In our Lord's name, these words I pray.
Amen.

A Reason

Everything happens for a reason.
The ups and the downs,
The changing of the seasons.
And as I look back at what's happened to me,
You just can't change your destiny.
It's not going to matter if it's wrong or right,
If you sat there and waited, or if you put up a fight.
The same thing will happen to the woman and the man,
You'll still be affected by the master plan.
Like the rising of the sun or the falling of the tide,
You can never change who you are inside.
And that's the way that it has to be,
You can't escape life's destiny.
That's why everything happens for a reason,
Like the rising of the sun and the changing of the seasons.
So sit back and enjoy the ride. Try and
laugh more then you cry.
And like the setting of the sun and the changing of the seasons,
We were all put on the earth for a reason.

Christ Came Back

Christ came back according to plan, Expecting
to find goodness in the hearts of man.
But everyone he asked, that passed him by on the streets,
Refused to give him shelter or something to eat.
He was finally arrested and put in jail, Nobody
would believe him or post his bail.
The bullies beat him up, He was bruised and cut. The
guards caught him preaching and they told him to shut up.
He was finally released and put back on the street, That's
where he finally died for lack of something to eat.

God Made Man

God made man,
Then he made woman,
He told them to get along,
To be nice to one another.
They had children and they told them the same thing.
Families developed into nations,
And these nations developed certain rules,
Religions, laws, and morals,
But they didn't always get along.
They didn't always listen.
And that's why this world, at this particular place and time,
Isn't even close to perfect.

The River

As I stand beside the river, the water flowing by,
The wind gently blowing through the trees.
I can hear my Lord a calling, calling from the sky,
Saying that he's coming back for me.
He's coming back for me, Lord he's coming back for me,
Saying that he's coming back for me.
As I stand beside the river, the water flowing by,
The wind gently blowing through the trees.
I can hear my Lord a calling, calling from his thrown,
Saying that he's come to take me home.
He's coming back for me Lord, he's coming back for me,
Saying that he's coming back for me.
As I stand beside the river, the water flowing by,
The wind gently blowing through the trees.
I can hear my lord a calling, calling from the sky,
Saying he'll be with me when I die.
He's coming back for me, Lord he's coming back for me,
Saying that he's coming back for me.
As I stand beside the river, the water flowing by,
The wind gently blowing through the trees.
I can hear my lord a calling, calling from up high,
Saying I'll be with him in the sky.
He's coming back for me, yes he's coming back for me,
My Lord and Saviors' coming back for me.

Being In Love

Being in love should never be painful,
There should never be wants or needs.
Unfulfilled expectations,
Jealousy lust or greed.

Being in love is a blessing,
It's sent from heaven above.
There should never be cursing,
Nor hit, pinch or shove.

Being in love should never be painful,
There should never be wants or needs.
Unfulfilled expectations,
Jealousy lust or greed.

Love should never cause any harm,
The heart was not meant to bleed.
There should never be shouting or screaming,
The other not forced to concede.

Being in love should never be painful,
There should never be wants or needs.
Unfulfilled expectations,
Jealousy lust or greed.

Love should always be tender and kind,
It should faithfully warm the heart.
It must streangthen and shelter and bring peace of mind,
And should never be torn apart.

I Understand

I really think I understand why a woman needs a man,
And a man does all he can to find a wife.

When God spit upon the ground then stirred the mud around,
And with his mighty breath he brought Adam to life.

Then with a rib from Adam side he formed
a woman as Adam's bride,
He named her eve and Adam took her as his wife.

Ever since that faithful day, through
both of them had gone astray,
Man has longed for a woman to abide.

He feels complete with a woman by his side.

Outside the Christian home I roamed

As I strode aside the hedgerow,
A collage of bush and trees.
A living web of plant life,
All twigs and limbs and leaves.

I could then see how the gardener
Had kept them all in line.
By cutting off stray branches,
And shaping them with time.

So this family of foliage,
Grows there strong and tall.
Serving its friends as a beautiful fence,
For foe's an impenetrable wall.

As I strolled aside the Christian home,
Between the house and that green wall,
It occurred to me quite suddenly
That there's really no difference at all.

Walls Of Sand

Erect your walls of sand to protect you from the sea.
The tide is quickly rising and the waves beat steadily.
Those who stood before you washed away some time ago,
But here you stand today, not knowing when or where to go.
So if you build your house of sand on the shore beside the sea,
Remember to lay plans to escape life's destiny.
The sand you lay that's hear today, tomorrow will be gone,
And if you want to stay, you'd better shovel all day long.

Get Out of the Sand, Stand on the Rock!

So Different

A woman is so completely different from a man.
I don't think men could even begin to understand.
They are so completely different in every single way.
The way they look, the way they act,
And even what they say.
I have no idea what God was thinking
When he created us this way.
Who knows?
Who cares?
I only know it's always been this way.
We're probably better off this way.

A Hearse

I got into a Hearse that crossed my path one day.
I looked inside, and almost cried, a man had passsed away.
I wished I could've told him that that
was how he's going to stay.
He said to close the coffin lid, he liked it better that way.
I wish I could've told him that is how it's going to stay.
I asked if I should say a prayer, and what he'd like me to pray.
He said it didn't matter, and he'd like whatever I'd say.
I got out of the Hearse, and watched it slowly pull away.
I wish I could have told him, that it's always been that way.
And that's how it's going to stay,
For everybody,
Everyday.

Our Covenant

Lord, help us in our covenant,
To live as Godly men.
Keep us and protect us,
And deliver us from sin.
Each one of us is human,
Which causes us to stray.
Lord, guide us and protect us,
That we may find our way.
Without our Lord and Savior,
Our hearts were full of strife.
But, since you came and died for me,
I have eternal life.
Lord, help us and protect us,
Please, change us from within.
Help us all to find our way,
And to live as Godly men.

My Body Is Tied To Me.

I'd like to do what's different
Than what my mind reveals to me.
I'd like to see beyond my sight,
That my eyes distill for me.
I'd like to feel more than a touch,
Which my skin deciphers for me.
I'd like to know more than I should,
Than this world teaches me.
O' curse my limited feelings,
O' that my body would quake.
Through the passage of time
Towards the end of the rhyme,
We all would hope to escape.

Who We Are

It dawns on me that throughout our lives we
have never actually seen Who we are.
When we look at our reflection, it is in fact
the exact opposite of our Appearance.
When we presume to know what others see, the
perception is always Jaded in some way.
Their presumptions and prejudices filtered through
what we've led them To believe and see.
When we sit back and look inside ourselves it is even worse,
As we clutter the vision with both our
assumptions and our fantasies,
Of not only who we presume we are, but
who we think we should be.
It is safe to say that we will never really
know what we look like,
Or what we appear to be.
It is only GOD almighty, our creator, the one who made us,
Who can truly see us both who we are,
Who we were,
And who we're really supposed to be.

I guess that's why he sent his only son to save us.
Because if you asked me or anybody close to me their opinion,
I'm sure they would see things differently.

I Can Feel

I can feel the blood
Flowing back into my veins.
My heart seems a little less frozen
And my mind has gripped the reigns.
Slowly, life returns again,
And I can almost see,
Now that I've been forgiven,
And you're finally returning to me.

Hearts Profane

Those with hearts, that are profane
And shout out, "Jesus Christ", in vein,
Are cursed by the Lord of hosts on high.
Their souls are damned and this makes the Angels cry.
Those who utter, "Holy shit", or angrily
shout, "God damn it!"
Will surely burn when it comes to Judgment Day.
Their souls are lost and will suffer come what may.
So be repentant while you speak, and
always careful what you say,
For all these words with which we curse,
Are the same words with which we pray.

I Think

Anyone who says, "Jesus Christ", in
vain, is guilty of blasphemy.
I think people who say, "Holy shit", have
blasphemed the Holy Spirit.
I think that everybody who says, "God damn it", are
guilty of trying to Command the will of God.

I think, in the end, the greatest tragedy of all mankind is...

I loved you,
I protected and provided for you,
You betrayed me.

So Many

There are so many people,
So very many people on earth.
I think I would faint
If I saw how many people that there really are,
And were.
So very many people,
Like stars, there are so very many stars.
I think I would faint
If I knew how many stars there really are,
And were.
There are so many things,
So very many things that I don't know.
I think I would faint if I knew all that there is to know.
And it occurs to me quite suddenly,
God must be really very old.

Chapter 8

Short Stories

A Tree In Gods Garden`

Once there was a tree in Gods garden
that had become distracted.
The fruit fell off, the leaves turned brown and piled
high above its roots, all but one. A woodsman whose
job it was to collect fire wood began to hack off the
dead twigs and saw away the rotting limbs.
And as he was about to cut off the last limb which held
the last twig that held the last dying leaf, an angel of the
Lord appeared and stopped the woodsman saying, "Do not
destroy this tree, for as there is still one leaf that the tree has,
she may this day decide to turn her attention upward, and
when she does, God will surely give her all she needs to once
again flourish". "Yes," the woodsman said. "I, above all
people, understand, that where there is life, there is hope."
With that, he gathered up all the twigs and limbs and leaves
and carried them away to be burned,
leaving not a trace of what once was
and what should never be again....we hope.

The Good King's Cup

It was the good king's cup that no one could touch,
Made of pure gold and emeralds and he loved it so much.
His grandchildren shouted as they all bounded in,
"Please tell us the story of your cup once again,"
As the last of the little ones found a space next to him.
The king took a sip from his cup and held it up to the light,
He gazed at its beauty then he grinned and said "all right".
"It was a long time ago, way, way back in time,
When none of these things that you see here were mine.
I was lost in the desert and could not find my way,
When I happened to find an odd cup thrown away.
It was tattered and covered with some hardened clay,
I thought 'this is useful, I may need this someday'.
So I picked up the cup and I put it away,
Then carried on with my journey trying to find my way.
In the desert, a stream that was there
was now dry, and I thought
'This is it' and that soon I will die.
But suddenly somehow, and I'm not quite sure why,
I thought 'dig with the cup, its well worth a try'.
So I started to dig in the dirt that was dry,
And soon water gushed up and I started to cry.
I filled the cup up, right up to the brim,

I drank and I drank, again and again.
I filled myself up and felt quenched from within.
I thanked God for that cup and every day I still pray,
'Thank you God for this cup, it saved my life that one day'.
So off on my journey I continued to roam,
though I had found direction, I still had not found a home.
And that's when I noticed the cup had a chip,
so I picked off the piece and found a diamond in it.
I couldn't believe it, what a surprise,
A diamond was gleaming right before my eyes.
So I marched into town that was there on my way,
and traded that diamond for someplace to stay.
I was completely happy and needles to say
that clay covered cup once again saved the day.
"Tell us more tell us more" the children said with a shout,
"tell us more of this cup you've been talking about."
"Well all right then, calm down,
There's not much more I can say,
as you know I only drink from this cup every day,
and slowly but surely the clay just wore away,
and exposed this gold and emerald challis
That you see here today".
"And that's why this cup is right by my side,
and here it will stay until the day that I die".
His queen leaned over and gave him a kiss and said
"Darling I just love it when you reminisce.

A Really Old Lady

I saw a really old lady sitting on a park bench smoking
Unfiltered cigarettes while feeding the birds.
She'd smoke them right down to the very end, pinched
between her boney nicotine stained finger and thumb.
She'd use the end of one to light the other, dropping the
first at her feet. She'd watch it smoke on the ground
while taking another long drag off her freshly lit
cigarette before crushing the latter under her foot.
A collection of crushed cigarette butts mixed with the bird
seeds at her feet. It was 7:00 in the morning, She'd stay until
noon then be back again the next day to feed the birds.
God willing.

There was an old lady who lived in a shoe.
She was so fucking old she didn't know what to do.
She buried her husband her family and friends.
She sat there and waited and hoped it would end.

A Young Oak Tree

A young oak tree asked the old castle one day,
"May I please lean my limbs on your wall?"
It seems that the wind is too strong for me,
And I fear that I may break and fall.
"Of course you can rest here"
The old castle then said.
"Lean on me whenever you like."
"You're welcome rest your limbs
On my stone walls,
Anytime day or night".
And as the years went marching along,
The oak grew big and strong.
And in order to pay the old castle back,
The oak held the walls up when the enemies attacked.

Chris Heigl

A Handsome Raccoon

A handsome and clever raccoon
Strutted about the forest filled with pride and ambition,
Constantly looking for excitement and pleasure.
Once he found a shiny silver ring.
He put it on his wrist and never once took it off.
After a time his wrist and hand grew with age
And he found that indeed he could not remove the ring at all,
But he paid this no mind since after all,
He was so handsome and clever
That this only magnified this fact.
Another time he came across a bell on a string,
And after slipping this around his neck,
He found he was unable to remove the bell.
However this also did not bother the raccoon,
Since indeed he was so handsome and clever
That it only announced this fact.
One day the handsome and cleaver
raccoon came across a fallen tree,
Which had a shallow hole carved out
some time ago by a woodpecker.
In the hole was a shiny coin that had been hidden therein
By a raven and had been long forgotten.
Spying the shiny coin, the raccoon reached in to grab the ring,
And as he made a fist around the coin
and attempted to remove it,
He suddenly found that he could no longer withdraw his arm.
As he struggled, the bell around his neck sounded,

Attracting a hungry bear. As the hungry bear drew near,
The handsome and clever raccoon tried
even harder to free his arm,
Although refusing to let of the shiny coin,
And the bell around his neck sounded all the louder.
This then drew the attention of a hungry wolf.
As the wolf and the bear drew even nearer,
The handsome and cleaver raccoon could see
That indeed he was in great danger,
But still he refused to let go of the shiny coin,
Deciding instead to try his hardest to free the coin
Until the very last moment.
As the hungry bear and the hungry wolf drew even nearer,
The handsome and clever raccoon thought it best to let go
And run up the nearest tree to safety before he could be eaten.
So he let go only moments before the
hungry bear and the hungry wolf
Were to pounce on the handsome and cleaver raccoon.
And as the handsome and cleaver
raccoon released the shiny coin
And withdrew his hand, the silver ring
on his wrist became stuck,
Trapping the handsome and cleaver
raccoon, and he was eaten.

The moral of the story is, whatever you cling to,
Either in the past or in the present, may well be your demise.

When I was a rabbit

When I was a rabbit, I ate wild succulent flowers,
All that I could find from evening until morning,
Saving the stock well above the root
So as not to destroy that which had given me life.
Then when I was a sheep then a goat then a cow,
I lived the same way, it was my nature.
Then when I was a wolf I would take the slow,
The old and the sick, as much as I needed.
The same as when I was a lion,
Then a hawk then a crocodile,
It was always my nature.
In this way I grew strong, as did the family of my prey.
Now that I am a human,
I do not need to follow the rules of nature,
Or even my own kind.
I consume all that I can find,
Taking as much as I can for myself until it is utterly gone,
Even to the detriment of my own health,
Until I am utterly dead.
Then I am buried and put into the ground,
And will someday be fed on by the flowers.

A Head Strong Spider

A head strong spider that hadn't eaten in days,
Finally turned to prayer and this is what he prayed.
"Lord give me something big to eat, so I can eat for days and days, Something I can feast upon in Jesus name I pray".
Then suddenly a moving tree or a gigantic upside down stump,
Tangled in the spiders' web, he'd trapped an elephant.
"O thank you" said the spider "it's just so hard to believe,
You heard my prayers and answered it,
so much and so suddenly".
The elephant herd what the spider had said,
And a tear welled up in his eye.
He understood what all of this meant
And he did not want to die.
"Be reasonable" the elephant said, as sorrow covered his face.
"I'm far too big for you to eat, and so
much would go to waste."
The spider thought for a moment,
Contemplating what the elephant had said,
He looked at the poor helpless pachyderm,
And imagined this poor creature dead.
"I've heard what you've said" the spider shouted,
"And though God gave you to me,
I've decided that I will have mercy on you,
So I'm going to let you go free.
"O thank you" cried the elephant,
"Your kindness I can never repay,
And I'm sorry for leaving my dung near your home,
I hope you can keep all the flies away.

Chris Heigl

We Stepped off The Train

We stepped off the train and onto the still wet streets
Of yet another unbelievably old and gloomy town,
Somewhere between the middle of the night,
And way too early in the morning.
The rails of the tracks flexed and bowed
As the train lurched forward,
Then slowly started pulling away from us.
One passenger car after another, dipping slightly to one side,
Finding the rail beneath it bending downward
As the weight of the wheels compressed
The rotten wooden railroad ties.
We hurried off the station platform
And down the flat stony walkway
That led to the shelter of the train station.
We tactfully leaped over the inky black pools of water
That perforated our path.
Looking more reminiscent of two fleeing gazelles,
Than two very tired backpackers.
Mercifully the rain began its downpour
Only after we'd reached the entrance
To the long arched hallway
That led to the station entrance.
Our footsteps echoed back and forth through the corridor,
Mixing with the sounds of a now driving rain.
That's when I saw the man,
Sitting with his knees drawn close to his chest,
His shoulders covered with a thin white sheet.
He was huddled with his back against the wall

Not quite shivering from the cold air
Pressing into his wet clothing.
He looked up as we passed by.
And as I did, I saw the face of the man
Whose likeness has been recreated,
Painted and sculpted thousands of times over.
Starring back at me was the face of Jesus Christ.
I was startled by the resemblance
And would have liked to have looked longer,
Had we not reached the doors of the station.
I opened them and let my companion hurry in
And as I looked back, I discovered that the man
Had vanished.
I paused, and then went inside.

A Mother And Her Daughter

I saw a mother and her daughter
and her daughter walking side by side.
Each one looked like the other,
Their hair their skin their eyes.
The mother said to the daughter, and not so casually.
"I hope someday your daughter treats
you just like you treat me".
Then the daughter said to her daughter, almost naturally
"I hope you have a daughter that treats you like you
Just like you treat me.
And so it's been from the beginning of time,
Like a well-known verse in a nursery rhyme.
The same simple curse so well-rehearsed,
That one will treat the other,
A little worse than they did their mother.

The Tiniest Kitten

The tiniest kitten who had just snuck away,
Then found and brought back for the third time that day,
asked momma cat if she still loved her,
And this is what momma cat had to say.
"Of course I still love you and I always will,
For although you're such trouble, you
make my life such a thrill."
"For Whenever I wake from one of my naps,
I of course find you missing and now bring you back."
So I think for a moment before I search high and low,
And ponder to myself at your age where I'd go."
"Though I've had many kittens, and I love every one,
I love you the best for you keep me so young."

A Greek Battalion

A Greek battalion was on its way to reinforce
the regiment that had become besieged while
defending the city against an invading force.
It happened that the commanding officer who
was quite pompous and arrogant had a pebble
lodged in his boot. A boot which he had
woven with thin gold ribbons and chain.
After some time on the march, the irritation of this pebble
on the commanders foot became more than bothersome.
So he halted his men and tried to carefully remove his boot.
The delicate knots and bows however would not
budge and they were far too valuable to cut, so
he commanded his lieutenants to devise a plan of
action to remove the bothersome pebble.
They all had differing plans, some brilliant, some
not so brilliant, but all to no avail. So the lieutenants
conferred to their captains who fared the same. Soon
every able bodied man came forward, each with
differing views, all to no avail.
This drama dragged on into the night and again into
the next day, when suddenly news came via messenger
that the besieged regiment had been solidly defeated
and the attacking forces were now at that very moment
just over the hill advancing at a steady pace.
Upon receiving this disturbing information the
commander rose up, gave the order to retreat
and promptly ran, pebble and all,
in the direction he had come.

Your Whole Life

You can spend your whole life looking
for something that isn't there.
Seeking the answers to questions that haven't even been asked.
Giving all your attention to something
that doesn't vaguely matter.
It's not a hopeless quest, though. Eventually, someday,
you'll find what you're looking for. You'll take what
you've found and weigh it against the time and
effort you've spent obtaining it and then determine
whether you've wasted you're whole life or not.

The Humans

The humans have breached the foothills, and soon a torrent of houses will come pouring down upon us. Great walls of buildings will rise up, some twice larger than the old oak trees that they devour in their path.

Standing here on the crest of the taller, steeper hills, one could follow the ebb and flow of man as he washed upon the shore. Slowing rising, advancing like a steady tide, flooding into the lowlands and plains.

Within the time it takes to grow from an acorn to a sapling, mankind had consumed the land surrounding the sea.

Form the time it takes to grow enough to be solidly rooted in the earth, man had conquered four times more.

In the time it takes to cast a large shadow on the ground, man had completely flooded the valley.

He spread tar as thick as a stump across the ground, erected colorless masses too week to withstand the common elements for more than a few dozen seasons. Nothing grows there within by those strange plants and trees, enslaved and put in there captivity for the good of that mankind.

Mankind has trickled in past the valley before, cutting a path, leaving it bare to the earth, establishing footholds made from the very trees he had cleared around him. But now, mankind has utterly breached the foothills and is soon to cascade over each and every living thing. Nothing shall be left alive in its wake. Their mighty yellow machines lay waste to all that stands before them. Not one tree is stronger. Not one animal is any fiercer. The earth lay exposed, ripped open. The tops of the hills are used to fill the gouges in the earth. Masses of soil moved here and there to flatten the landscape on which only weeds are let to grow before the ground is covered with smooth rock and tar. Nothing shall grow there again except those that have been planted by that mankind.

You shall never again have the joy of losing a seed to the wind and having your kind grow near you. Diversity will never be allowed within this kingdom of iron and clay. There will be destruction of the natural world will be complete. No more will your leaves pile thick above your roots.

No more shall your branches rise unbridled towards the sun. And even at death, no more shall you dissolve back into that place whence you grew.

Look now, the humans have utterly breached the foothills.

These Cells In Me

I've got all these cells in me.
From top to bottom I am a collection of living cells.
If I divide the skin a number of cells will escape.
White cells, red cells, fluid.
Removed from the body they die,
Become dry and blow away.
All dead cells dry up and flake off.
Rarely missed be the rest,
Never even noticed for their individuality
Or all the good they had done for the body.
These fluid cells of mine, moving freely from here to there,
Each knowing what to do and where to go.

At night I look out over the landscape
And see red and white lights,
Like cells moving to and fro,
Coursing through the veins of the city.
Each one free to go here or there,
Fulfilling a specific duty until the day they die.
Then they dry up and blow away.
Rarely missed by the rest,
Never even noticed for their individuality
Or all the good they have done the body.

A Man

I knew a man who basically slept all day. He'd get up
only to feed or relieve his body. If he wasn't asleep in
his bed he'd be asleep in a hole he'd worn in his sofa.
There was known a man who basically worked
all day. He'd got up early to finish what he'd
started and stay up late starting something that
would need to be finished the next day.
A well-known man devoted his life to studying basically one
Thing. If he wasn't studying it, he was
collecting it, cataloging it,
Lecturing or writing about it.
These men all had wives whose lives were
basically devoted to their children.
The more children they had the more
time thay had to devote to them.
These children were similar to their parents
and basically did the same thing only a little
differently and a lot more efficiently.

Closer You Are

The closer you are to someone,
The freer you feel to hurt them.
You would never insult a stranger,
Yet you yell and scream at your children.
You would never hit an acquaintance,
Yet you feel free to slap your wife.
And the one you hurt the most of all,
Is the one who's closest to you.
The person you harm the most,
Is yourself.

So Tell Me

"And so tell me, what is it that you
have learned up until now?
What is it that you can repeat to some stranger
about what your life has taught you
up until this point in your life?"
"Life, my life has taught me that every
choice that I make has consequences,
and those consequences have ramifications that
stretch well beyond my own boundaries
and even time itself, effecting persons whom I may know,
and people whom I may never know. All directly related to
my particular diction to which I was responsible for making
at that place in time."
"So you're saying that you had an effect on people?"
"I'm saying that by me being alive, I have an effect on people.
And this effect may influence many or
few, in the immediate future
or in some far away happenstance that only time will know."
"And that's all you have to say?"
"Basically yes, in short, choose wisely."
"Wisely?"
"Yes, in good conscience."
"Conscience?"
"Yes, according to your inner self, your nature, your soul."
"Soul?"
"Yes! The part of you that determines what's wrong
or right, what's good or bad, evil or Godly."

"Godly?"

"All right! By making the decisions that God would have you to make in your life at any given time, at every given moment, for every purpose on Earth and in plain view of Heaven so that things in your life, my life, will go according to some perfect plan that will result in me not screwing everything all up and resulting in some catastrophe of some kind, either now or in the foreseeable future, There, are you happy? I said it. Follow God's precepts and try as you might to do his will and you might not distort what is designed for you."

"Designed for you?"

"Stop repeating the last sentence of every paragraph!"

"Sorry, but it is puzzling."

"What's puzzling? Don't smoke, don't use alcohol, don't use drugs, don't have sex out of marriage, don't lie, cheat or steal. Don't kill or do any other number of things that will hurt yourself or others. You know all the things that we, you and me, do practically every day if we can?"

"So in other words, be good to yourself and your fellow human?"

"No! In other words, be as good as you can possibly be or else the repercussions will definitely come back and bite you in the ass!"

"And this is what you've learned up until now?"

"Fuck, yes!"

"Good for you! Anything else?"

"Yes, falling in love with a bad woman produces good children."

"Funny."

A Tiny Pebble

A tiny pebble viewed the world from on a mountain top.
A boulder sat below it, tasked to hold the pebble up.
"I rule the world," the pebble said,
"no one is higher than me,"
"I supervise throughout this land, from sea to distant sea."
One day, as nothing stays the same,
The wind and snow and driving rain,
Threw both the pebble and the boulder
down the mountain side.
The pebble moaned and groaned and wailed and said,
"I truly want to die."
Until the bolder softly said,
"Now please, dear pebble, don't cry.
Our lives have far more meaning here,
Now let's hold this mountain up high".

A Giant Stone

I thought I recognized a giant stone within a brook.
It reminded me of something, so I waded in to take a look.
The water was quite frigid and moving faster than I thought.
I could barely keep my footing as I
struggled to reach that rock.
The sandy bank had fallen away and the water
had reached my chest, Now, seemed the time to
swim for it, or at least, I thought it best.
So, against the current my arms did fly,
And with all my strength, I tried and tried.
But, that giant stone eventually eluded me.
And as I reached the other side,
It was then, that I came to believe,
Life's not all about achieving ones goals,
Sometimes, it's about the journey.

Chapter 9

Narratives

Weapons

Weapons are for those without mercy,
Guns are not made to forgive,
Vengeance and anger and hatred,
Will poison the homes where they live.

Bitterness breed's thoughts of reprisal.
Reprisal sheds light on revenge.
Revenge is for those who are spiteful,
Being spiteful will indeed be your end.

For those who forsake forgiveness,
Whose memories focus on the fight,
Whose intentions conceive to annihilate.
Will never know wrong from right.

Tar In My Lungs

I have enough tar in my lungs to pave a road.
Not only am I dying but I live to kill myself.
I see time a nature's winepress and I'm drinking to my health.
Toxins, anti-toxins, bio feedback and the like.
Decay for life is nothing but decay,
And all the while with a smile
I slowly pass away
. Like dry brown grass or wheat's beaten chafe
We are but for the moment and then we are the past.
I have heard that we are travelers,
Guests on God's green earth.
Where then is the afterlife?
Is our death rebirth?

I've Never Killed

I've never killed anything large before.
I've yet to clean up a pool of blood,
Sever a head from a limb,
Portion the meat to appropriate size,
Or remove excess fat and skin.
Though, not long ago, as most of us know,
There would have been a list of things for killing.
But, not now, and I say it's better this way,
More time to be spent consuming.
We are consumers you know.
From the Dawn's early light
Until the Evening's soft glow,
Everything we do is consume.

I've never been at war before.
I've never had to kill a human,
Take a life to save my own,
For God and country,
Allegiance sworn.
I'm not familiar with war,
And all its gruesome gore.
Though, not long ago, we fought with our foe,
Enemies until the end.
But, not now, and I say, it's better this way.
More time to be spend consuming.

I Knew A Butterfly.

I knew a butterfly.
She wore the colors of a rainbow,
Her skin, softer than her soul.
And she knew every child that was ever born.
She painted each and every one with smiles and giggles.
She was always warm.
It was never dark or raining,
In her, there was no scorn,
Nor condemnation or berating.
And this was her home.
It was always populated by the beautifully frustrated,
And every time they'd cry,
A tear would well up in her eye,
And she'd smile at them,
And she'd tell them that she'd be their friend,
From now and through tomorrow
And until the end.
I knew a butterfly.

Terror

Terror,
What the hell is terror?
All my life I have never known,
This feeling I have never shown.
Terror.
Pure unfiltered terror.

Apparently, through the centuries,
One group hates another,
Enough to drive the other into extermination.
In the hopes of purification,
Justification for their annihilation.
Terrorization.
What the hell is terror?

I remember feeling fear and fright,
Being afraid of what bumped in the night.
But, what I have never felt,
Is my capture,
My ensnarement,
my restrainement,
Containment.
My life has never been held
In someone else's hand.

I would like to thank God and Country,
For making it possible for me to be free,
Especially, for protecting me,
From terror.

Those people

I do not like those people,
And they do not like me.
They are not at all the same as us,
They act so differently.

They never show as kindness,
Because we are not their kind.
We do not feel or act the same,
Their attitudes are different than mine.

This is why there is prejudice
Because they are not at all like me.
It's been this way from the start of time,
It seems the curse of all mankind.

That's why I don't like those people.
And why those people don't like me.

Wars

Wars are best fought
With ill intentions
And no discretion.

Fights are best won
With younger men
And a better gun.

Victory is best achieved
When one side chooses
Not to grieve.

Peace is best attained
When love abounds
And hate's restrained.

The Last Time

The last time I was here, things were different, my Dear,
The grass was always greener, the sky was always blue,
The water was much cleaner the last time I saw you.
But, here I stand today, and I can barely find my way,
I cannot even walk in a straight line.
Nothing has survived the wrath of time.
The last time I was here, our closest neighbor was a dear,
And we would spend our time enjoying life together.
It seemed the day would last forever,
Since the last time I was here my Dear.
But, now, nothing is the same.
Our lives are completely rearranged,
I see only you when you kiss my lips goodbye,
And in the evening when I come home
And you say, “Hi.”
Things have changed so much it makes me want the cry,
Since the last time I was here, my Dear.

The Fire Reaches For The Sky,

The fire reaches for the sky,
The drum beats out of time,
The mystic healer's anguished cries,
"Purge the evil spirits or dye".
The drum beats out of time.

The fire reaches for the sky,
The EKG sounds out of time,
Tests and data we'll analyze,
"Purge the cancer cells or dye".
The drum beats out of time.

The fire reaches for the sky,
White ash on their face and thighs.
The entire room we'll sterilize.
The doctor says he's going to die.
The effected one tries not to cry.

The fire reaches the sky.

Here I Am,

Here I am,
Once again,
Lying down on the sand by the sea,
Where I'll be,
Till the tide brings the water to me,
To cover me,
To carry me,
Then I'll open me and I'll see,
What will be?
And what I see,
I can never remember,
When the tide has surrendered,
And the waters receded,
And the night's been repeated,
And I open my eyes to the sky,
Once again,
Here I am,
Laying down on the sand by the sea,
Where I'll be,
Till the tide brings the water to me....

A Flag Waves.

There a flag waves.
Not a rag on a line
Blowing free in the wind,
It's a flag waving.
Attached to a pole,
Handled by few,
What does it mean?
What shall we do?
Is there some great meaning?
A warning in fact?
Is it someone distressing?
Are we under attack?
Is that our flag?
Shall we rally to greet it?
Or is that there flag?
Should we hide ourselves from it?
Is it red? Or red white and blue?
Is it warning us what not to do?
I wish I knew.
Look quickly there,
Another flag waves too.

Run And Jump And Play,

I used to like to run and jump and play,
I'd do this each and every day.
But I am different than before,
I do not do these things anymore.
Why that is, I cannot say,
I guess that part of me
Is gone and passed away.
Why? I really cannot say.
I used to sing and dance and create art,
And all my poems I knew by heart.
But, all these things I used to do before,
I haven't time to do them anymore.
Time and troubles have let my talents
Slip away, and why that is I just can't say.
And, now, I feel that part of me is gone
And passed away. Why? I really cannot say.
I've lived so may lives and each one is different.
It seems that way each morning when I awake.
I wonder if it all was just a dream.
And as I struggle through yet another day,
I wonder what will become of me.
And how much more will I change?
I cannot say, because, that part of me is gone
And passed away. Why? I cannot say.

I used to have a business, I even had a wife.
But, because of my indiscretions,
God's removed these from my life.
And, so, I've changed my ways,
And I don't do that anymore,
And my life is so much different,
Then the life I lived before.
Why? I really cannot say.
But, that part of me is gone and passed away.

Pearls and diamonds

Pearls and diamonds and bands of gold-
Tokens of thanks for her labors.
She dolefully wears them as proof of her worth,
Gifts of love and trinkets of favor.
Compare with me your jewelry,
Place yours next to mine,
Have we a thing in common,
Have you a life like mine?
Pearls and diamonds and bands of gold-
All with an obvious reason.
Each one celebrates stories untold,
Life, love, and freedom.
Compare with me your jewelry,
Place yours next to mine,
Have we a thing in common,
Have you a life like mine?
The Pearl-
A symbol of life, giving birth,
Mother of my children.
The Diamond-
Great and valuable stone,
But valuable more are you.
Rings of gold-
Mark the beginning of time,
My happiness started with you in my life.
So, compare with me your jewelry,
Have you a life like mine?

The monkeys are on a tangent,

The monkeys are on a tangent,
And the workers have gotten loose.
The zoo keepers says he's lost his mind,
And perfects how to tie a noose.
The demons and the angles,
Are hoping for new romance.
It seems that everyone's gone astray,
Just one last chance for one last dance.
How can we live together like this,
When none of us are at all alike?
How can we enter heaven,
When all we ever do is fight?
The humans have discovered fire,
And now all they want to do is kill.
And the angles have discovered passion
And are enslaved by their own free will.
The zoo keeper says he's lost his mind
And won't allow another birth.
He said he's poisoning the food supply
And destroying the planet earth.
How can we live together?
When none of us are at all the same?
It's hopeless to search for peace of mind
When everyone is quite insane.

Primal UrgeTo Fight

There is this primal urge to fight when something isn't right,
When somebody has done you wrong.
The losers tend to be week and the winners tend to be strong.
It seems it's always been this way for the entire human race
From the beginning of time up until this very day.
We are going to get even so the victim's say
"Take up arms, set things right
You are obligated to get even."
It's an ugly human plight.

Justices and judgment and rules of the law,
They never satisfy the primal urge at all.
In the end, the victor, the one standing,
Is justified, while the beaten is quickly forgotten.
So throughout it all, the accused are abused and are beaten,
And the abusers, the winners of the fight, are right.

Sometimes I forgot

Sometimes I forgot what I know is true.
For instance there are billions of other people on this planet
Just like me called you.
Each one of us is destined to live, to laugh, to cry
And finally in the end we all, each one, must die.
And for all of this I ask myself the question why,,
And the answer seems to be we all, each one, must try.
Sometimes I forget that the sun dose not rise in the morning,
Nor at night will it fall.
In fact the sun does not move around the earth at all.
And its size is enormous, so big I recall
Someone saying that 10,000 earths could
fit within that big flaming ball.
Sometimes I forget that I'm a spirit trapped inside a body that
I call me. And when I try to see my reflection in the mirror,
I never see myself, I only see me seeing me.
I believe that's the same person that you always see.
Actually, as you probably know, that's not who I really am,
That's what I look like as this man.
Who I am you or I could never see,
Until I'm dead, that's when my spirit, the real me is set free.
And that's the way I'll look for all eternity.

This or that

I planned to do this or that and I longed to go here and there,
So I went here and there and did this and that,
But I found that after all was said and done,
It didn't matter that I did this or that.
And went here or there,
It simply didn't matter.
I've also discovered that doing this and that
and going here and there,
Not only does it not matter,
But nobody really cares.
So in the end it's important
That you are happy being here, where you are right now,
doing what you're doing today,
For your own gratification.
Because when you're done,
Nobody will care,
And it really won't matter.

Water

Water will always flow downstream with ease.
And as it joins with other tributaries on due course,
Combining turbulence with utter force,
Colliding headlong into rivers strewn
With rocks and trees. That torrent of water
Might think back to days gone by,
When rain drops fell down from the sky,
Combining gradually, it seemed, to inch
Downstream with ease. Not unlike a hurricane
That started with a breeze.

Opposites attract

Opposites attract its true,
But friends, true friends
Think and act the same as you.
It's almost as if you were always one,
You laugh the same,
You cry the same,
You share in what is fun.
The pain you feel
Will also make them cry.
And what you find important,
They too have always tried.
But overall, what makes you truly friends,
Is that they will love you,
No matter what, until the end.

The greatest mystery of life

The greatest mystery of life
Is not as complex as it seems.

It revolves around hope
And achieving One's dreams.

It's rooted in joy,
Contentment and health.

It's not found in fame
Or fortune or wealth.

The answer to life's mystery,
Is being happy with yourself.

I wonder what I look like.

I wonder what I look like.
I wonder how I'm seem.
I'm sure the way I see myself,
Is not how you see me?
I wonder how I look,
Through the reflection in your eyes.
If what was true came shining through,
We both would be surprised.

Never be too sweet

Never be too sweet or the world will gobble you up.
Never be to bitter or the world will spit you out.
It is never a good idea to be on fire for this or that,
For you are certain to burn out quickly, and those
Nearest you would not stand to be too close to you.

Utopia,

Utopia, my world. Utopia, your world.
I never really use my legs to get around.
Though, I move faster than the speed of sound.

Utopia, my world. Utopia, your world.
People hear me speak a thousand miles away,
You can read my every thought each and every day.

Utopia, my world, Utopia, your world.
It's utterly amazing, all the things that I have seen,
and looking back, I find in fact, it all seems like a dream.

Utopia, my world, Utopia, your world.
Electronic database, megabites and RAM.
I can fly through cyber space. I'm virtually subhuman.

Utopia, my world. Utopia, your world.
E-mail me, anytime, day or night, or we can meet on Myspace.

I am Afraid Of Spiders.

I am afraid of spiders.
I kill each one I see.
I fear that they will cause me harm.
Inflicting misery.
One day I killed a spider.
That came to close to me.
And I wondered if that arachnid
Was as afraid of me.

Ethnic diversity

Ethnic diversity,
Political changes,
Religious freedoms.
The salt in the stew of our Government.
The right to an abortion,
The right to bear arms,
The right to free speech.
Bitter vinegar that dilutes the broth.
Family,
Security,
Prosperity.
The fuel that kindles the fire.
The right to an attorney,
The right to a trial by your peers,
The right to remain silent.
Fatty oily pieces of our Judicial System.
Commitment,
Personal sacrifice,
Good will towards men.
The finest pieces of meat in the pot.
The right to liberty,
The pursuit of happiness,
And justice for all.

Amen.

The tin Man

The tin man had a brain,
But wanting a heart is utterly insane.
And not knowing what's going on,
Is what made that straw man so strong.
And that lion without courage,
Was more humble than weak.
But Dorothy and her dog,
Wanted what we all seek.

Man in a circle,

Man in a circle,
Surrounded by men and women,
Set amongst the natural world.
Moving themselves over there,
Enlarging their circle out there.
Pressing their backs against the wall of nature,
Subduing, taming, and redirecting the elements.

Never leave the circle,
If you leave the circle you will die,
You will get lost and never find your way back,
Nature will kill you and the elements will devour your flesh.

Man encircled by land
Reaches out across the sea.
Take your wife, children and family.
Take from the wild, enslave the poor,
Find what is most prized amongst the natural world
And bring it back into the circle.

Never travel too far outside the circle,
You'll become marooned,
Captured by the wilderness,
Killed for your trespasses,
Dissolving into the elements.

Man circles the sun
Surrounded by the stars and galaxies,
Set amongst the universe.
Never travel too far outside the circle.

The State Of The Art.

The state of the art.
samples of humanity.
The state of the art.
compilation of history.
The state of the art.
Delegation of idea's.
The state of the art.
Tangible, intangible.
The state of the art.
Valuable, invaluable.
The state of the art.
Technologically advanced.
In every society throughout time,
Man has constructed a form of perfection.
Rich in color and texture.
Mathematically correct,
Esthetically appealing.
Forms and ideas communicated.

The state of the art.
Indication of advancement.
The state of the art.
Civilization pre-destruction.

The earth is flat,

The earth is flat,
The earth is curved,
The earth is round.
Oh, I've heard it all before.
It seems your soul will last forever.
The earth is green,
The earth is brown,
The earth is blue,
It's all been said before.
It seems that you will have eternal life.
The earth turns round itself,
The earth turns round the sun,
The earth turns round the galaxy.
I've not been here before,
But when I die,
I'll be here forevermore.

Pigeons

Pigeons, nearly twenty of them
Circling the house and I thought,
I'm as free as a pigeon,
And I like it that way,
I go out in the morning
And come back at the end of the day.
I eat in my cage but sometimes I eat out.
I'm not prone to violence and I tend not to shout.
I travel so far and so fast.
So incredibly close to each other
And we hardly ever crash.
They say that pigeons are not very smart.
Smart enough I'd say.
They like to get out in the morning
And come back at the end of the day.

People

People, there are so many people,
Hobbled here within Earth's constraints.
If I only knew how many people there were,
Chances are I'd probably faint.
Like stars, all those glorious stars.
Gleaming like diamonds in the sky.
If I only knew how many stars there were,
Chances are I'd probably faint.
And knowledge, there is so much to know,
With everything that's ever been done or said.
If I only knew all that was to know,
Chances are I'd probably faint.
With all these fascinations flickering inside my mind,
It occurred to me, quite suddenly,
That God must be older then time.

Lived in secrecy

So, all our lives are lived in secrecy.
We share what we want to
As long as we're not giving
Away anything important.
It seems to be along the lines of,
'Never lend a stranger your gun
Least that they may use it against you.
Interestingly enough,
Those that are closest to you
Are the one's whom the truth
Is held furthest from.
And those whom we barely know,
Are privy to our deepest and darkest secrets.

Time

Time is the consequence
of our conceivable events.
As we are aware, we conceive time.
If we are asleep, or unconscious or dead,
There is no time, and time therein has no relevance.
Therefore, the meaning of life does not hinge,
Nor revolve, on the passing of time.

The perfect woman

The perfect woman does not doubt her own beauty,
But, is far more concerned with her
hygiene than paint and perfume.
She holds tightly to her frugalness as
being her most valuable asset
She is creative beyond measure. She is caring to a fault but
not one to be taken advantage of. She never speaks ill of
others although her opinions are without argument. She is
kind to animals and children alike. She does not need a man
but lucky is the man, indeed, whom she finds favor with.
She seeks not envy, though envy follows her like a curse.
Oh, that she would teach the children. Oh, that she would
advise the youth. Oh, that she would care for the elderly.
Let the Lord above give long life to
her and all who are like her,
and may her offspring flourish and prosper forever.
Amen.

Hypocrisy

Hypocrisy is man's best friend.
We smile when we feel sad.
We frown when we feel glad.
We say we tell the truth- we lie.
When women feel happy, they cry.
From the day of our birth until the day
That we die, hypocrisy rules our lives.
Our friends, they will betray us in the end.
Our life long lovers, away we often send.
Trust me, is always what they always say-
But, all the while, they were plotting to betray.
From Dawn to Dusk, in every land,
Hypocrisy is the rule of man.

Like footprints

Like footprints in the sand,
Each step that we have planned
Leaves an impression,
So our path is clear to see.

If you open up your eyes and turn around
You'll be surprised to see the winds of time
Erode the prints we've left behind.

Apparently, it seems it's for the best.
The further you look back, the less
Distinguished is your track,
The perfect step blends in with the mistake.
So, in truth, what difference does it make?
Now, close your eyes again.
Face to the front and step ahead,
Pretend you know just where it is you're going,
And don't look back to much.
You're better off not knowing.

Who am I?

Who am I?
What am I?
Who is this that I see?
When I look into the mirror
Am I staring back at me?
Am I something more beside myself?
Is there something more inside?
Is the reflection that I gaze upon me or a disguise?
Do I occupy this body?
Is it me I really see?
Is this physical appearance
Who I'm really supposed to be?
I wonder who I really am,
I wonder all the time.
Am I something more than flesh and blood?
I wonder who I am.

You shouldn't be so angry

You shouldn't be so angry.
You didn't get it right.
There's some misunderstanding.
There is no need to fight.
A miscommunication,
A mistake of sorts,
Brought on this confrontation,
And instilled this state of war.
And as I said before,
You didn't get it right.
You are in fact mistaken.
There was no need to fight,
And kill,
And maim,
And wound,
And torture,
And destroy,
And annihilate,
And bomb, blast, shoot and burn.
It's obvious.
You didn't get it right.
You shouldn't be so angry.

Keep your head down,

Keep your head down,
Look toward the ground,
Walk straight ahead,
Don't turn around.
Try not to think,
Don't say a word,
Believe what I say,
Ignore what you've heard.
Walk ahead slowly,
Don't try to run,
This isn't a game,
You're not here to have fun.
Behave at all times,
You're no longer free.
A slave to the world
And reality.
Don't look to the left,
Don't look to the right,
Always be passive,
Try not to fight.
Someday this will end,
All too soon, I do fear.
So you best pray to God,
That there's no worse than here.

I don't think your right

I don't think your right,
Low I think I contest,
I judge, I disagree,
I have an opinion.
And not unlike a stray sheep
Separated from the flock
I will be hunted down
And killed for going astray,
For making my own way,
For the path I choose
Is untraveled, and those
That would seek to enslave me
Hide in the dark corners
And seek to end my life
Or at least insure it unravels.

Crystal

Crystal reveals its impurities
Only after it's been broken.
A diamond will shine it's brightest
Only after it's been cut.
Every piece of granite will reveal its history,
only after it's been sliced and polished,
Exposed for all to see
And every human show there character
Only after they've been tested.
Steel is only strengthened
After passing through the fire.
All temperament is fastened
Through hardships, pain and mire.

The Land Of 'OR'.

I'm living in the land of 'or'.
You're either like this or like that.
Things or thoughts or ideas or whatever.
It's either right or wrong,
Acceptable or unacceptable,
Informed or ignored,
Righteous or ridiculous.
I'm living in the land of 'or',
Which is inbetween the rock and a hard place.
I'm living in the land of 'or'.
You're either like this or like that.
Things or thoughts or ideas or whatever.
It's right or wrong,
Acceptable or unacceptable.
Informed or ignored.
Righteous or ridiculous.
I'm living in the land of 'or',
Which is inbetween a rock and a hard place.
I'm living in the land of 'or',
Illuminated by the sun,
Populated by fanatics on both sides.

Row, Row, Row Your Boat

"Row, row, row your boat, gently down the stream,
merrily, merrily, merrily, merrily, life is but a dream."

We get lost in the rhythm of the rhyme
And fixate on the repetition of the words
Losing the meaning entirely.
It should be,
Row your boat gently down the stream,
merrily, for life is but a dream.

Everybody knows it but nobody gets it.

Where is happiness

Where is happiness?
How can I find joy?
Show me the place that warms my heart
and dries up all my tears.
Is there some island of peace and comfort?
Is there some mountaintop that fear and worry cannot reach?
Is there some stream that quenches all my longing?
Will more money purchase peace?
Can I educate myself with some knowledge that will lead
me to elation? If I lay with another who is right and good
Can I absorb righteousness and goodness?
Maybe a pill has been made that can provide for all my needs?
Can a magician change me into a pious man
Free from the sins I've committed?
Is there a type of religion that will show me
how to attain eternal enlightenment and
power over my fleshly shortcomings?
So, these things I've pondered and let my mind wonder.
Suddenly, I realized the truth, which took me by surprise.
It seems I've known it from the start.
True happiness is right there in your heart.

You are all that you are

You are all that you are (I want to be near)
How near or how far (those that have love)

My religion tells me who I should hate,
Who I should kill for their sins.
My country exposes my enemies for me
And my neighbors judge me by my skin.

You are all that you are (I want to be near)
How near or how far (someone who has love)

My religion unveils who's wrong and who's right,
Who I should love and hate.
My family draws slightly closer to me,
And I desperately want to escape.

You are all that you are (I want to be near)
How near or how far (the one that I love)

My religion justifies warfare,
As long as our God's in the fight.
It doesn't matter who lives or dies,
As long as the stronger one's right.

You are all that you are (I want to be near)
How near or how far (the one who is love)

Row

Row, row, row your boat, gently down the stream.
Merrily, merrily, merrily, life is but a dream
And that's pretty much how life goes.
I've heard that insanity is making the same mistakes over
and over again somehow expecting different results.
We fall in love with the wrong person,
We choose the wrong occupations.
We make the wrong friends
Live in the wrong places.
Listen to our minds listen
To our hearts listening to others.
We block out the truth,
Block out the facts,
Block out the unknown,
Block out the known.
We want what we cannot have.
We get things we cannot keep.
We dream of things that will never happen.
And that's pretty much how life goes.
Mankind will always make the same mistake
Over and over again.

So row your boat gently down the stream.
Merrily, for life is but a dream.

Every beat of my heart

Every beat of my heart
reminds me that my life is slipping away
Every second and every minute and every hour of every day
I am reminded that my life is shorter
by each beat that ticks away.
And so I must remember to enjoy the life I live
Trying to be kind to live in peace and to forgive
Violence hate and prejudice take from me precious time
So to live a life that's filled with grace is to live a life divine.

It's your eyes

It's your eyes
It's in your eyes.
It's all the hope and joy and gladness
These things shine so brightly from your eyes
Everything you see is all a mystery
And all of life is a curiosity
You do not look you stair
And something's always happening
Either here or over there
Everything you are
And all you'll ever see
Is fresh and new and wonderful
It's your reality
And so you see there's magic in your eyes
All the hope and joy and gladness
For you every day is a surprise

Every chapter of my poetry

Every chapter of my poetry
Is an analog of the tragedies,
Analogy of the travesties,
Intricacies and simplicities,
Indignities and extremities,
The complexities,
And the immensity
Of the infinity
Of the history
Of my life.

Chapter 10

Short Narratives

Short Narratives

I can hold my breath longer
Than I can go without your love!

Learn to love, and you'll never hate yourself again.

Shower your lover with kisses,
And they will always grow founder of you

Holding hands, touches the soul

Sleeping in, accomplishes nothing.
Sleeping in each other's arms, accomplishes everything.

If you wake up and he's still holding you,
Shower him with kisses

The goal that has no finish line, is love.

Too much of a good thing, is always love,
And that's never bad.

If you said I love you every time you said my name,
I'd be happy for the rest of my life.

If there's any doubt in your mind, let me
show you I love you instead.

Short Narratives

If I love you just a little more every day
for as long as we both shall live, I just might get it right.

There's only one way I can tell you I love you,
But a hundred ways to show you.

They never said love was easy-
They said it was soft and gentle.

There's no such thing as tough love-
Only hard lessons taught by people with hearts of steel.

Your smile shines so brightly,
It always lights up my entire life.

I am blinded by my love for you,
Which is probably why I can't see being with anyone else.

If you live your life like an open book,
Nobody will judge you by your cover.

If you like it, that's good enough.

When your beliefs are rock solid,
Nothing can break you down.

When you bind your family together in faith,
Nobody can rip you apart.

Short Narratives

When you sink your foundations deep
in truth You become a pillar
unto the community.

Love is never easily rushed.
In fact, it often overlooks the races entirely.

Always be the first to tell your wife how beautiful she is,
Then don't be offended when everyone else agrees.

Giving your love to another
Is exactly like picking up a poisonous snake.

Admiring another woman is like studying the feathers
Of the poison arrow that you've
accidentally shot yourself with.

There is no use hiding who you are,
Everyone else can see you.

Being too sweet or to bitter
Will make people sick of you.

If you're known for giving cheap shots,
You're going to be considered a pain in the ass.

The goal is to get to heaven,
And be loved by those who know you there.

Love should flow like warm honey,
And taste just as sweet.

Short Narratives

Never hide your love
For fear of forgetting where you put it.

Love should never be put on the back burner.
Chances are it will go cold.

Anger put on the back burner
Will eventually boil over.

If you sprinkle a little love on everything in your life
It will never be bitter.

If you expect love to wait for you
Don't be surprised if it wanders off.

First and last impressions leave their
mark on everyone you meet
No mater low long you live.

Pain is soon forgotten but love lives on in the hearts
Of all of those touched by it.

Love is a seed that you plant in the minds of those you meet,
Over time their memories of you will be sweet and enjoyable.

Spreading love causes everyone to grow fonder of you.

I have put all my excess faith
In you.

Do not grieve
If you believe you will receive.

Short Narratives

If you going to build a wall around your life
Make sure it's high enough to keep the bad out
But not so high that you can't see when
to let the good come in.

Keeping all the bad things closed up inside of you
Also keeps much of the GOD from getting in.

If your planning on locking the door to your heart
Make sure you leave a key under the mat.

Love overlaps you neighbor's boundaries.

If someone steps over your boundaries,
Chances are they will step on your toes next.

Take responsibility for your own actions
Before offering to bury the hatchet with someone else.

Strategists usually revolve around the assumptions
That the opponent will make the first mistake.

If you assume something,
Chances are you're going to make a mistake.

Achievements always start with a gut feeling.

If you can control your feelings
You can steer clear of all the un-pleasantries
we tend to crash into

If people begin to have feelings toward you,
Make every effort to insure that there good ones.

Short Narratives

If you feel insecure-
Ask someone for a hug.

If you feel lonely-
Ask someone for a kiss.

If you feel incomplete-
Ask someone to marry you.

Always sit next to your spouse-
You never know when the opportunity to kiss might arise.

Dancing with the person you make love to-
Should feel relatively similar.

How is it that everybody wants what I've got-
When I've got none of the stuff that they've got?

If you give your heart to someone-
Don't ask for it back later.

If you give your heart to a careless person-
Don't be surprised if it comes back broken.

If you give your heart to the woman of your dreams-
Make sure she isn't a nightmare.

Fill your heart with compassion,
And you'll never be hungry for love again.

A fist is unable to feel love.

Short Narratives

If you give your heart to the one you're going to marry,
Give the rest of yourself also.

If you see a little bit or yourself in your children-
Assume the worst.

Make God the cornerstone of your life-
And build from there.

Life is exactly what it seems.

Good people don't suffer half as much.
Bad people suffer twice as much.

Whatever you worship-
That is your God.

Whatever you seek-
That is what you will find.

Whatever you say-
That is what you mean.

Whatever you believe-
That is how you will act.

Whatever you love-
That is what will love you back.

Short Narratives

Love God-
Because he first loved you.

Live for God-
Because he died for you.

The seeds of hope grow best when
planted deep within your heart,
And showered daily with generous streams of faith.

Hope is generally routed in the rocky soil of hardship.

If you stand for truth-
You will never fall for lies.

Words can cut deeper than sharpened steel.

Hope can be dashed on the rocks-
But, unlike dreams of grandeur, can never be broken.

Where there is life, there is hope.

Put your hope in tomorrow-
But you faith in today.

If you believe-
You're off to a good start.

Whatever you do to them-
They will do to you.

Shallow thoughts
from an empty mind
I wade therein from time to time
And though my thoughts are really not that deep
Its awlfully hard to drownd in them
When thay only cover my feet.

I dedicate this book to Adam and Sabrina Heigl with special thanks to Keli Carpenter. I love you.

chrisheigl@att.net

Printed in the United States
By Bookmasters